Cloak &
Dagger Butterfly

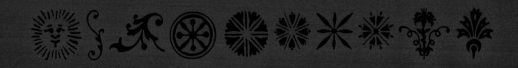

Amanda Eliasch

Special thanks

Ryan Belmont Designer
Rushka Bergman Stylist
Caroline Brown
Jack English Photo Editor
Enrico Navarra Gallerist
Joanna Russell Copywriter
James Rann Copywriter
Alexandra Shipp Assistant
Alexander Webster Photographic Assistant
To all those assisting the assistants.
Julia Laverne
Danielle Moudaber
Chad

Published by:
Chipmunka Foundation
4 – 14 Tabernacle Street
London
EC2A 4LU
United Kingdom

http://www.chipmunkapublishing.com
Copyright © 2008 Amanda Eliasch
ISBN 978-0-9560436-0-3
Printed in the UK by Howitt Group

This book would not have been possible without the support of Enrico Navarra. He and I have been working together as great friends for three years. We started with a project called Made by Indians, followed by an exhibition of Indian Artists on the beach at St Tropez (encouraged By Dr Jean-Louis Sebagh, my then-boyfriend). Enrico and I were neighbours, and he flew in his helicopter to my house in St Tropez most days. He and his girlfriend Laurenc gave their moral support to my email poetry-words last Christmas. We have also done another project, Made by Brazilians, which comes out later next year. Enrico's enthusiasm and charisma make working with him a wonderful drug that you can't say no to. The foregoing words were inspired by a myriad of conversations and connections with some great girlfriends – and one or two fabulous men – but this book is dedicated to all men everywhere, especially those I have loved, those with whom I am currently enraptured and those I have yet to meet. (If I don't love you, you must have done something terribly wrong.) Thanks also to all the models – who speak for themselves and only work for me until they have signed their Hollywood contracts – and to the make-up artists and hair stylists who made them look so ravishing.

My thanks to insomnia.

Any similarities to real, existing situations are figments of your imagination.

My thanks to Blackberry, Eurostar, the Costes Hotel, Tamara de Lempicka, Tatler, the Daily Mail, the British Film Institute, the BAFTAs, Oscars and Nobel Prize, my mother, my aunt and Daisy the cow, Phentamine, Lexomil, British Telecom, the space beneath the clock at Waterloo and two discreet drivers, one gone but not forgotten, the other forgotten and not gone. For photographic inspiration, I am indebted to Michel Comte and Bob Carlos Clarke; for funny times in the darkroom to David Vellor (even though he has sent me to Coventry); and for the rest to curling tongs, Mac red lipstick, YSL platform booties, convertible cars and a pair of skinny jeans. I have neither watch nor sense of time – it's always NOW – but any structure in my life I owe to Red Bull, crumpets and Marmite. A special mention goes to Sue Lash, for two hours of individual lash-fixing a week. And to all those who are anonymous, this message: I am saving your reputations and sparing your feelings.

In memory of my Mother Mrs Caroline Brown nee Gilliat.

The Passion Chain

I had been considerate,
I had been compassionate,
I had participated
In remaining
So docile and
Passive.
Addicted
To the passion
Of being
Disappointed.
Love jumps out at me
Like beams of light,
It's the
Same light that
Accompanies
Its pain.
How could he not
Recognise
My map of senses?
I wasn't shocked
To see him.
I didn't have the time
To feel if he
Cared
I had hesitated
As he left the room,
And quickly
Thought I would
Book myself

Into new
Hotels.
I saw him
At art gallery
Openings
Although he wasn't
There.
It was as if he
Had
Whitewashed his
Soul, scrubbed it
Clean, as if to make
Himself
Squeaky clean.
I saw his name
On invitations to
His shows
But didn't go
My
Breath would
Remind me of
His breath and mine
In tune.
I love my teapot set
It's delicate china
With tiny fractures
I thought about past conversations
"Sometimes you need
A memory"

I thought I had memories.
"No, you need
Something real"
He had said.
I choked
Realising
Why would he love me?
I doubt if any man
Could?
Why should they?
As
I believe that men
Are there to
Torture me.
The English
Can never go to the
Heights of
Ultimate
Passion and love,
Where it can go to
love and hate.
You see I was like
The child he wouldn't
See.
It was just his
DNA
He had said.
Unknowingly
He had jogged

The pain of my
Past.
I had never been
Able
To give a chain
To my daddy
"I love my papa".
As he had around his
Neck that day.
I had so wanted
To be loved
When I was
Young
And free,
But the damage
Was done you see.
As I wrote
My mother spoke
To me.
And for the first time said
"You so
loved your
Father,
You used to
Say
"Dat's Dada's nose"
And grab his
Chin,
And fling your hands

Around his knees
With ice cream down
Your face.
But when he
Threw you across
The room
I had to leave."
I had nothing
More to say
To her.
I knew I could never
Love her as I should,
I knew she had only
Been able to
Tell half the truth.
I did have one chance
To hold his hand
Before he died
In a mental hospital
In the USA
I put his hand in mine
And realised they
Were the same
And thought:
I will look for
Somebody who has
The same hands,
As his and
Who fits mine.

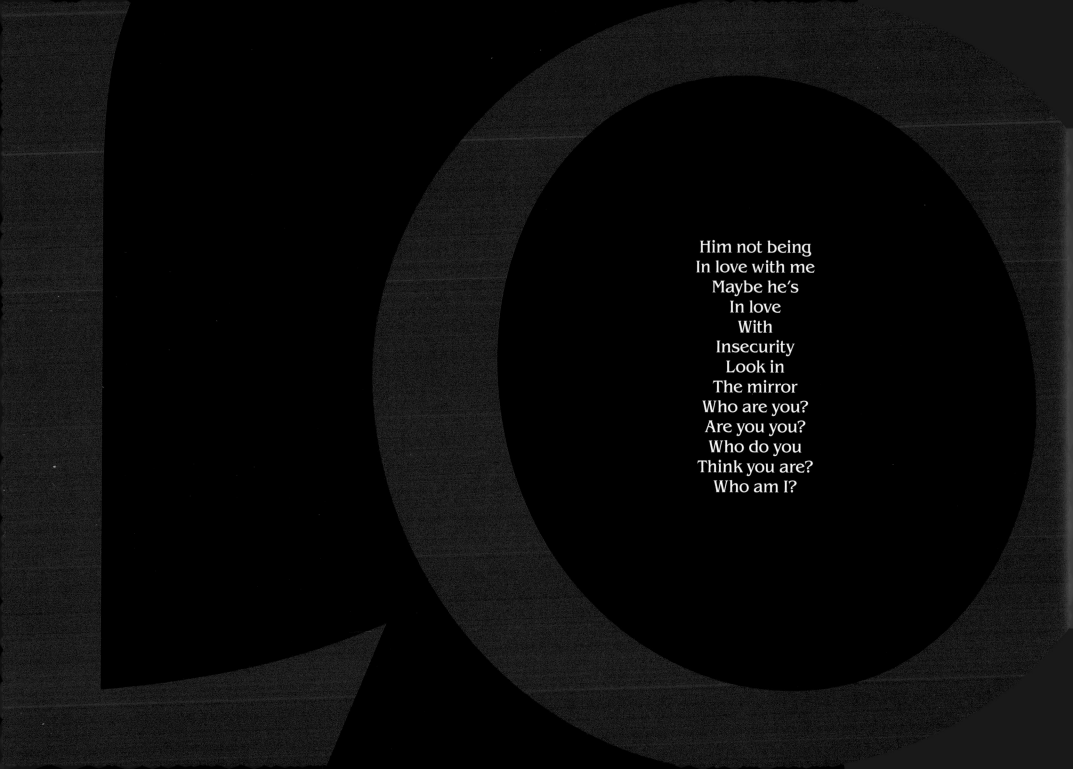

Him not being
In love with me
Maybe he's
In love
With
Insecurity
Look in
The mirror
Who are you?
Are you you?
Who do you
Think you are?
Who am I?

Pink Ditties

He came to me
Laughing
Saying I had overwhelmed
Him
Frightened him
Disturbed
His thoughts
I had relaxed
And written
Ditties hundreds
Of pink flowered
Ditties
Bent double
Not able to speak
I grabbed my
Knees
Rocking
Wanting to be
On my own
And held
All at once
He said he had
Confused
His fantasy life
With his reality
Shocked
Flattered
Frightened
Dismayed
I knew I loved
Him

In that second
I hadn't considered
It before
Not really
Please please
Leave me
No don't
I wanted to be
Loved again once
More
Unable to speak
Tell the truth
So
I say I can't live
With anyone
Have to be free
Not to leave
His wife
His family
That I could hate
Him if he did
Hopeful
Fearful
Unable to speak
Unable to think
Slowly saying
That I have to
Live a life
Of truth and lies
Finding knowing
The difference

The tangle
Muddle
Searching always
Searching
Seeking
My truth and knowing
My lies
All he says is shhh...
I say nervously
Let's end it
He says that
It would be
Inappropriate
At this time.
Weird strange words
Do you want to...?
I look up,
He hesitates
Putting a scarf
Around his neck... ,
Putting sunglasses
On
Although it's dark
Outside,
A pair of black glasses
Hiding his eyes
His soul,
I see them though
His eyes
Vaguely through his
Mask

As he looks at me
Hesitating. Firmly
Saying
No,
I look down
Looking up
Slowly gasping
I speak,
Absolutely not
Expecting nothing
Expecting everything
We hold time together
For just a second
My reality his
Fantasy
Him
Saying there was no
Future,
But I you see
Live in the
Present
My fantasy reality
Truth and lies
Altogether...
I grab his finger
Did I?
Holding his sculptured
Body cheeks nose
One last time
But it's late
There is no

Time to
Explain I hate
To talk...
Remembering
His words
Minutes seconds
Before
What do you want
Me to do to you
Pleasure slipping
Lick you
Lick me
Here there
Kiss me. No you
I feel his body
Biting me biting me
Adoring me
Removing pins
The fresh air calming
He leaves
I know he loves
Me I just know
As I sleep
With a pillow between
My knees rocking
Myself trying
To remember
What
Was said
A pen
Holding small

Delicate sweet
Memories in my hand
His smell
I know I love
Him
I remember fleeting
Seconds
Why did I say...?
I couldn't live your
Life
I can't do ordinary
Giving him
The opportunity
To say
I can't live with you
I say
I have to be free
To see the earth moving
Flowers changing
Ice forming
Wanting
To be sick
Nervous
My make up running
My hair like straw
My curls destroyed
I lie to save
Him
I lie to love
Him
I lie

Little Pearls

I love truth
And yet resort
To many lies
To see
If other friends recognise
Their charms
The greatest problem
For me
I think is boredom
It is the worst feeling imaginable
Although interested
In everything
From doors to cement
There is nothing
More deadly than
A sour cold
Relationship
Driven by society
Or duty
I am driven by pleasure
And am happy
As long as I am harming
No one
I cultivate, grow and
Dream of receiving and
Giving this, and realise

It is my true love
I have had teachers, but
Through
My many
Mistakes have
Taught
Myself,
I am in love with life
And air and pearls of wisdom.
Reading philosophy is only as interesting as
Reading a thesaurus, when we are young
We are taught how
To behave and what we
Will receive if we do
as we have been told,
It is interesting to watch
How often our teachers
Were wrong.
I like to see and watch
Myself make
Mistakes
Or not
And laugh
And cry in turn
But be free of
Another's ideals.

The Train

Dark
Dressed in black
I sit on
The train
Not knowing
Why
For years I have
Sat on the train
Black glasses
Tired
A coat
A book
And dreams
Not knowing
Why
How
Where
I dream
Continual movement
Dead
The rolling of time
I close the shutter
Hoping to sleep
My legs
Crossed
And why I'm

Here I don't know
The sound rolls
Me forward
Forward to the
Unknown
Excited
Unexcited
I think
Close my lips
And grit my teeth
What went
Wrong?
Me no yes
Don't lie
Pretend
Just be
As curious as you can
The rolling of the train
Don't talk please
Please don't talk
And remind
Me
Of a
Life I wish
To forget
A book unread

The Prison of Life

You are changing
Into a beautiful
Wild animal,
Caged for sure
But still wild.
You are like
A lion pacing up and
Down, with bars in front
Of you and the knowledge
Of what it was like
To wake up with
Elephants and zebras
Like a hawk,
Waiting to land on
Its prey
Hungry and patient.
Waiting and waiting for some
Small delicious
Creature that is
Succulent to rip
And split in two

To reveal its
Insides
To see if it would
Bleed
And give up its
Bones for you.
Pacing, feeding,
Killing, eyes alert
The nostrils
Filled with desire
To smell the wind
Your muscles strong
Compact eager
To leap
And run.
Your hair up on
End ready to escape
The dreaded
Concrete cage
With metal bars.

If The Telephone Doesn't Ring, I'll Know It's You

He hasn't called.
I love him.
He doesn't realise
How much.
Will he call again?
To touch me
To hold
And bite my
Neck
To rip
Me open
And kiss my
Hair
To pull
My nipple
And stroke me
There.
Nothing.
Maybe he doesn't
Care,
Maybe his life
Has trodden
Onto his heart
And nailed him
To

The children.
Paperwork
Tax return.
He said he never
Said he loved
Me.
I didn't care.
I did.
I didn't need
A
Return
But the silence
Deafening
Silence
Hurts
Me
I long for his
Thick black
Hair
The smooth
Soft skin
And no
Pain
And no despair.

Tell me the top six pleasures
Of sleeping alone,
I can't think of any…
Thought so…
But as you hang upside down
On a branch
It's different for you,
And the coffin isn't big enough
For two

Yellow

Mornings
I like silence
Please don't talk
Don't speak
Let the darting
Yellow Butterfly
Rest

Chocolate Coated Kimono

Arrived,
Japanese
prepared
kissing
I realise
I know nothing about anything,
I'm in love,
He loves me
I think,
The way he touches
The way he holds me
The way he cares
Attention to detail
A teapot
Silver
On top larger indentations
On the bottom smaller

The music, the quietness
The Kimono
The peace
The hands
Something about him is so perfect
The insecurity
His insecurity
His ambition
What am I?
Am I real?
A butterfly?
Or am I real?
The touch
The kissing deep
Swallowing
Mournful
But am I real
Engulfed in
Pleasure

Addicted to
His hair
Silky, fine
Black
Noble
Beautiful
Melancholia
I don't want to
Sleep
We are so long cold dead
In a grave
I am alive
Free
And able to meet
This strawberry
Chocolate
Man

the Mac

ness

The madness
Slipped
Inside me.
Me mad
Or him?
Me truthful
Or him?
The madness
Me or him
Him or me?
It slipped
The courage
The lies
The soul
It slipped
And died
The greyness
The rubbish
In the street
The early
Morning
Rising
The soul slipped
And died?
Or was it the
Truth?
With no
Lies
Forgive her
Forgive me
The velvet tongue
The cloud lifted
What is this?

This and that?
Forgive him
The iciness
That drove him
To this
Or that
The coldness
The banter
The nagging
I love you
The nagging
You love me
The endless
Boredom
The day to
Day
Trivia
The window-cleaner
The Hoover
The illness
The school run
The bank balance
The dreary
Black days
The pram
The idle chatter
To press repeat
No
No
To rise from
This
To be free
For the rose

Coloured freedom
Of
This and that
And laugh
And love anew
And cry
And feel
And not be choked
By the cloak of smog…
And therefore
Forgive me
Forgive her
Forgive him
And clear his
Soul from
This and that.
And make the passing of time
With fresh and happy
Tunes.
And
Time will forgive
All
And understand
The dreary black
Life
Was not for him and me
And me and him and her
And let the
Natural cycle
Of life
Begin
And time will
Forgive.

House Or Hat

Love is not a
Designer label.
It's not a house
Or hat
You can put
On and off.
It's
Seldom convenient
It's not a clock
A scientific fact
Nor a particular
Colour.
You meet
In unlikely places.
The odds are worse
Than the lottery.
It's painful
It's elusive
It's not guaranteed
When you lose it
It's the most painful
Thing
On the planet:
Nothing is more
Dreadful
Than lost love.
Nothing

Can replace
That person –
Only that person
Can drag you from
Your bed.
It doesn't come
In measured cups
It's elusive
It's not consistent.
I want to be free
And yet you don't want
To be a fragment
Of somebody's life.
A love story has
To be without
Conditions
To have fresh air.
You don't want somebody
To make you feel better
Or to make you sob.
The terrifying thing
Is what
You liked about the
Person
Is the thing you
Hate in the
End.

Don't Make Me Stale

Don't make me
Stale
I could resent
You for making
Me bored
Give me harsh
Honesty
To lie to
Your soul
Is
Worse
Than infidelity
It gives
No
Meaning to any
Story
To be a fraction
Of a man's life
Leaves me
Listless
I wish

To be the sun
The moon
No
Stories
Clean
And honest
No matter
How ghastly
Their truth
Is
Don't waste
My time
I just wish to
Be a light bulb
So
Activate all
My senses
Take
Risks in
Every breath
You take

Help me
Make my
Truth yours
And
Don't lie
Don't look back
It looks so
Black and white
But life is grey
It rains
No need
To hurt
Anyone
And
No-one to hurt me
I want the peaceful
Solitude of an
Egg-timer
And the wildness
And freedom
Of a bird.

Stunned

Stunned
Depleted
I left the bed
I had been
So full
Of joy
An hour
Or so before
Happy to
Share what
I had seen
Quietly
I left
Pretending
I knew what
He had
Meant
He was
So slippery
Like an
Eel

And me
What you see is
What you get?
Is it over?
I lay there
Calm
Observing
From another
Sphere
I looked
To the table
Spare
Like a monk
A few unread
Books on a
Few great
Men
And a little box
Saying
Find Lucy.

Don't Go
Dear Friend

Head hung
Low the
Cup fallen
Eyes
Sunken
Blood dripping
No
This was
My friend
My love
My piece
Of gold
Now
So lowly
On
A
Stool
Before so
Merry
And happy
Laughing

Now
With a
Debauched
Cold look
What had
Happened
To my goldilock
Child?
The one I
Loved
And tickled
So quick
She had
Been
Laughing
An hour ago
With my hand
In hers
She hadn't
Spoken
She didn't cry
For me
Near the end.
I knew.
Precious creature,

Anything
I can do?
Can you hear me?
Please wake
Please
And dance
With me
And play
With toys
And ride with
Me and fish.
Wake wake!
Don't go
Speak
Don't go
Friend
Can you hear?
No
Too late
Goodbye my pretty
One
Goodbye.

One Day
I Will Laugh

One day I will laugh
At this
In the sky
Loved but not enough
In the sky
Alive
Not knowing why
Oh yes I do
Hoping but afraid to hope
Longing but not longed
For
In love
So in love
I leave my bed like a dream:
For something for nothing?

Will I know
The answers soon?
To why I am here
On the plane
To see to hope?
To see love
To hold
Maybe?
Maybe not
But I can dream
What he thinks I don't know?
I am mad?
But all will be clear soon
When I am old?
I will remember
This moment in the sky

Blindfold

Blindfold on and so to sleep
Eyelids closed
The train moves
On
Shut out the world
And do not eat
Try not
To talk
Wordsworth
And dream of
The time we
Met
So close on the train

Fresh Start

Collapsing in
A pool of pity
Is no good
Straighten the
Back
Clean the teeth
Brush the hair
Put on my war
Paint
Your never know
Who you will meet.
Go for a run
Take a kip
Walk by a lake
Hold a hand
Pick some flowers
Stand in some sun.

A Man
Who Knows His
Destination

A man
Who knows his
Destination
Is dull
Is this life?
To know who you are
To know why you are
And what?
Should we,
Should we not
Feel anxiety
To choose to live
To change
To live and frolic
To enjoy the wind and grow
With choice
A man who knows his
Destination
Is a dull man.

Alien Arrival

Why am I so
Tortured
Affected by
What people say?
How would they
Know that before
They speak
Their words
Have been told
To me
Already by
An alien
Arriving on
Hidden electric
Waves
To my brain.

How would a
Person understand
That before
They speak
I already know,
And see what
They see,
That I wear
The cloak
They wear,
Of dandelions
To be blown
Away
Petals of a daisy
To be pulled
One by one

He loves me,
He loves me not,
He loves me,
How could they
Know that their
Words shock
Me
And leave me
With their broken
Desire.
That
Their thoughts are
Like the wind and
Change within the
Hour.
How would they know?

Show Girl

I have had to
Compromise
Too much
If I have to
Plant gentle kisses
On his buttocks –
Why?
Unless I love him,
Why would I want
To do this ?
And why would
I want to
Love him half way?
Am I mindless girl,
A show girl
In a kick routine?
Shall I murder my
Feelings?
It is agony.
Should I sever the
Umbilical cord?
Or should I allow this
Fiend to grow
To feed from
My bleeding
Heart,
Smelling his skin
Licking every droplet
Of his
Sweat.

The Early

Morning

The early morning
Cold
The church bells
Distant
An
Empty bed
So looking forward
To
The ruffled
Pillows
An unmade bed
And
What?
I don't
Know
I had hoped
to be...
The empty cupboard
Open
The coat hangers
Gone
But have no
Clue
One is working
The other dead
I once loved him
Too
I shall hide
The broken
Wings
The stomach
That
Tells it all
The dreams of
Youth
Long gone

The running in the
Fields
The picking of berries
The hay barn
The racing dogs
The choir
I used to laugh
I shall be married
To a Duke
And live
In a castle
The saddle clean
My boots
Polished
The spurs glistened
In the wind
The hair net
The clarinet
The hunt
Galloping on
The Marlborough
Downs
The books
And
Shakespeare
All gone
So happy
One week
And dead the next
Sad and alone
The birds
The trees,
I knew them all
And I long
To hear
Sounds
Of life

Long-gone
Remember
The music
The hellish lessons
Practise
Screaming
Through my hair
The uniform
The band
The marching through
The streets
The changing
Of the guard
And discussing
Henry VIII
The treble clef
Practised
On every book
The flowers
The nettles
Should have told
Me
That life has
Twists and turns
I had dreams
Of palm trees
The Chinese
The deserts
And the Indies
But in the end
All I really
Wanted
Was the intimate
Sound
Of the man
I love.

What's It All About?

What's it all about
To gyrate and dance
What's it all about
The sticky
Fucking
Nightclubs
I hate
The drinking, smoke and
Noise
The social
Fucking talk
The crap
The drugs

What's it all about
This sticky
Fucking
Nightclub
That is such hell
The swearing
The fake
The bongo
Wongo
The billy willy
And the silver snake
The wobbly
bottom
The gold buckle
The young fucking idiot

In the loo
Sniggering and sniffing glue
Conscious and unconscious
In his poo
The fucking nightclub
What's it all about?
It's not because
You dance you can't
It's not because you grope, you can?
This is my
therapy to hell.
I hate this fucking culture
To hell.

Will I Like His Hidden Side?

Will I like his
Hidden side?
Will he like mine?
His rejection
His bad moods
The butterfly
A given cup
A squirrel
A mouse
He thinks he hasn't
Given enough
For a connection
Lies
He thinks he isn't
Enough
With a book on
Meditation by his bed
Even if he cuts

Himself off
He says he
Stops himself
From saying
I love you
But yes you have
You have told
Me before
I never told you I love
You
Yes yes
For now
I may have mentioned
I love you
Its all word-play
Depending on
Punctuation

Elixir

Here's your daily elixir,
You didn't have to sell
Your being to me,
You just had to stop making
Me into a vampire,
I didn't ask for your blood,
I just asked for
A pound of flesh!
I can be deadly nightshade
Belladonna or
A hot tomato or
I could be a potato but I
Haven't a jacket
You put
Me to your lips
Sucking blood like
A cigarette
Then you discard
Me and trample on me on the
Floor like nicotine.

I
AM
IN
LOVE

I am in
Love
But
Don't know
Who
With
I will travel
The world
For skin
And smell
Swim
Breast stroke
Across the
Atlantic.
If I have to.

It's Flattery, Not Praise

It's flattery
Not praise
When I write
To you or give
Myself to
You
I just wish you
Would
Impart something
To me
Open the door
Send me a note
Remember
My birthday,
A bunch of flowers
Would do
Just do it for me
Help me
Bring my shopping in,
Load the dishwasher
Clear the table
Clear the garden
Walk nearest the pavement
Protect me
Are there any men left?

Real ones
That know not
To show me the menu
With the prices on it?
I don't expect
Presents
Diamonds or a car
A sweet note will do
Little gestures
A box of chocolates
A CD of some
Music I don't know,
A walk in the park
Hand in hand
The emasculated
Man
Is not attractive
Have women
Done this?
Have they?
So
Say thank you
If a man smiles
At you
And
Smile back

If they dare ask you out
Don't tread on
Their hearts
Anything they do
For you be
Loving and grateful
Giving to them
Selflessly
And expect nothing
In return
Don't be an accountant
And nag
Starting
A sentence
With
"After all I have done
For you"
Give freely
Playfully and light,
We own nobody
And control
Nothing
Freedom is trust
And trust is
Freedom.

And I So Wanted This Man

I so wanted
This
Man
Curly
Haired
So difficult
And quick
To find
A
Fault
So cheerful
And happy
To please
I crept
To him
So early
And
Said

Goodbye
To
Things Injections
Turned
My head
The clever
Needle
Piercing
And
Now
I see
The tongue
So cruel
Without
A care.
Can't you just
Die with dignity
He screams.

The Breath

The moments
When I
Leave
Are hell
On earth
A fusion
Of
Confusion
And passion
A magpie
Did I see a magpie?
No
No thank god
A blackbird
I wonder if
I said too
Much
Talking talking like a
Parrot
Repeat
Parrot
Maybe too
Little...
I shall not speak
Ever again
I will listen
Listen and learn
Did I lie
Was I a coward
Speak the truth

Did I speak the
Truth?
Was I silent
Interesting
Correct
Better
Feathers
Glowing
Light
Can anyone
Anyone tell
The passion
I've had?
Too often
Too much
Is said
The aimless chatter
In the bed
Shhh...
Quiet
Listen
Dream
Think
Feel when
And really
All that counts
Is the breath
A rat in a cage
All thoughts
Rush through

My brain
Hot and cold
My hair
My make-up
Running
The pins
So many lost
I had been
So happy
And now return
To ordinary
So ordinary
Not for me
Ordinary
Dust
The smell of polish
Tea
Pillows
I grab
All that
Feels
Familiar
Telephones
A friend
I grab at straws
I remember
I remember
The silence
And
The breath.

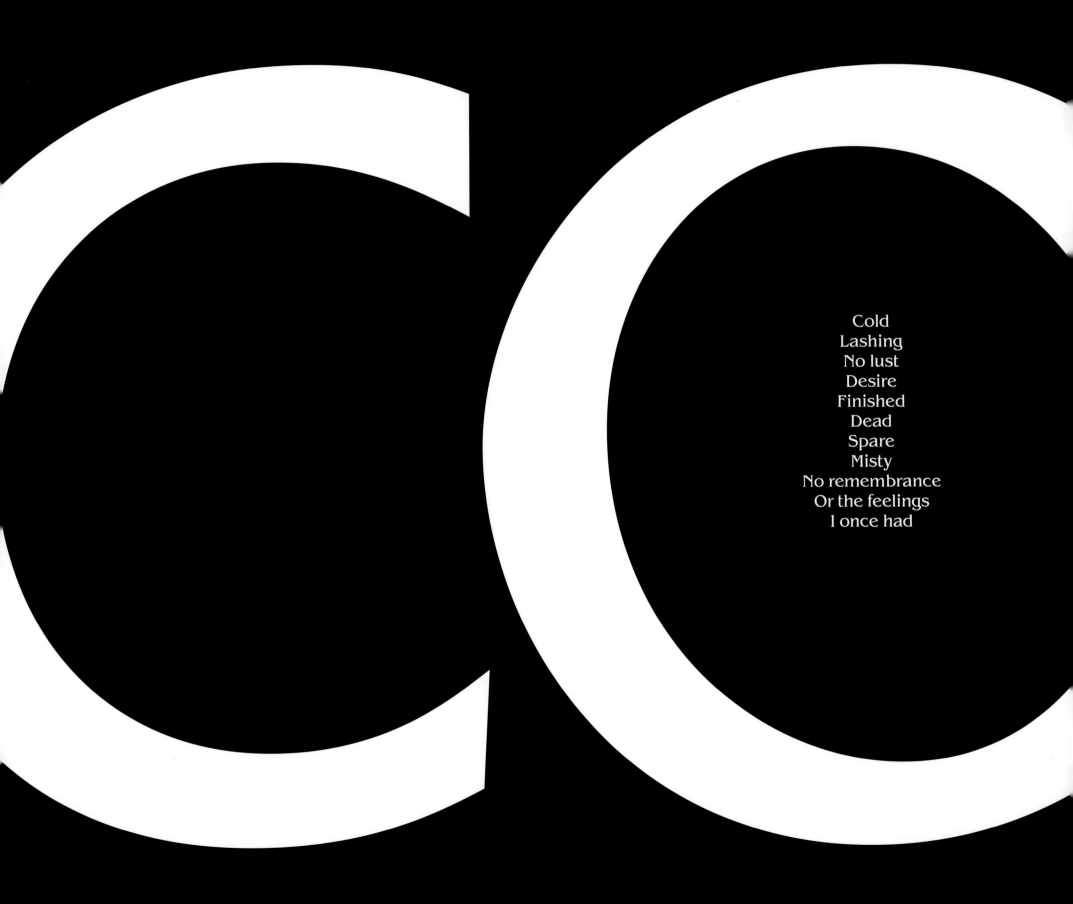

Cold
Lashing
No lust
Desire
Finished
Dead
Spare
Misty
No remembrance
Or the feelings
I once had

Dead
Desire
Dowsing
With
Death
Deluded
Sanity

Tired

An
Old
Fool
I still
Believe
In love
So tired
Of sleeping
Alone
Pretending
Wanting
Dying for
Love
To be held
Adored
So alone
Sunday
Alone
Waiting

First Thoughts

I liked her
She gave me looks
Of hate when
I looked at her
She doesn't want
Anything other
Than to be loved

Hot Pebbles

Hot
Pebbles against
Skin,
The wind gently
Crossing
My
Neck
Softly, so softly
Dreaming
Of time
Spent
Frogs croaking,
Dolphins swimming,
Ants marching
In straight lines
Sand
Following a
A salty taste
Meditating watching
The palm trees
Sway.

DON'T
SAY
A WORD
PETER

Don't say a
Word, Peter,
I think,
Creep out
I feel danger
I smell it
I don't want
To lose
This man.
This man
On who I had placed
Such unfounded
Hopes
Just a dream
On a train,
His charm
Had
Taken hold,
The elegance
Once there
Drained,
And me
Laughing
Like a whore
Spread on a
Bed, unloved,
For
No reason, other
Than his guilt.
"Were you unfaithful
In your marriage?"
He asked
His beauty drained,

Before my face,
And reality on
View.
He was
Married
And me divorced.
And
Divorced in some
Ways for him,
Why I don't know
Cruelly turning,
The answer
Well I don't know
He scolded
And then
"I should have waited"
For what?
For you to regain
The ability to lie…
You don't understand,
I thought
I like truth, real truth
Ugly, raw,
Truth
He lies
He escapes
He thinks?
His reality on view
His monk-like ways
"You have to go"
Yes, I thought and quickly
"Wash"
Why make beauty
Sordid?

Why cheapen
His butterfly?
Her golden wings
Bent
I loved this man
I love his dirty brain
But
There are limits.
I checked
His door dirty,
Unloved
Arrogant
He thinks he can lie
To himself?
Let him kid himself
He never made
Love?
I don't believe this
"You were sunshine
Today in the train"
And ended
By text
So cruel
And me so in love
And a question
Is asked
Is this for real?
Please God please
If you hear me
Give me this
Wonderful
Man.

Real ?

Is it real
The ecology dream
No plastic
Does it dissolve
In the earth?
Knives
The war-torn world
Where do all the bullets
Go?
The
Rubbish
Spit, blood, and
Shopping
Bags
The drugs sedate
Us
Sellotape to
Keep me quiet
Fumes from cars
Radios blaring
Pop music thumping
In my head
Babies crying
Rock, chewing gum
McDonald's
A five minute
Lunch
Drugs, morphine
Injections administered

To the nearly dead
Thailand,
The beautiful prostitute
The beat
The rebel spitting
Rocky-horror
The smells of
Burnt toast
From
The council house
Estate
Brixton
The frizzed up hair
The violence just before
Bed
Plastic teeth in a jar
Hairspray, Vim and
Bleach.
The old woman
In care,
Her children
Just stare
The press advise
Spend, spend, spend,
A new T.V.
Computer the
Old one dead?
Where do they
All go
The refrigerator

Bones
And flesh?
Where do they all go
Recycle they scream
The out of work
Recycle
They
Claim.
Buying the latest iPod
Radio
Car
Throw the old one
Away
Buy a new one in
The private jet
The grand hotel
Eden Rock and the fast
Set
The plastic boats with
Gallons of petrol used
Durex in, bad sex out,
If not
Where does all
The rubbish go
A pit?
A stream?
A river?
Endless logging
Six billion people
So lots to

Feed
And lots
With no
Welfare
Endless queues
With no bread
The sewage
Does it melt
Does it disappear
Or go like
Fumes
In the air
The politics
The men in grey suits
Do they really care
Children on rubbish
Dumps
The wells dried up
And new insects
Everywhere
Dirty hospital beds
And the
Ozone
All but gone
Bad teaching
With no playgrounds
Look what we
Have done
To our exotic smelling
War-torn world.

The Sounds Of The Sea

The sea gently
Touches the stones
Incapable
Of silence
It comes
And goes
The bird talks to
Me
Asking questions
I won't answer
Nagging
I can't understand
I try to
But am lost
Does he want me to
Look?
But I don't see
The lemon-grass
Tom yam goong
The shadows of
The trees

Mirrored in pools
Of water
Green
An Eden
Amongst swaying
Palms
I rest my head
And dream
Against Thai music
The ancient
Instruments
Calling me to wake
To think to speak
The bird calls
Again
I block
The sounds with
Thoughts
Of any place
My brain never
Sleeps
But I am alone
With the sounds of the

Sea
Changing in time
With the
Wind
Colours bright
And dark
From blue to yellow
It never stops
To wait
Or think
No
It is free
To dance and call
Like the birds
I don't
Understand
But I am alone
To discover
The sounds of the sea.

Sand

Sand
I have a problem with
Sand
Loving deserts, beaches, egg-timers,
Morning eyes,
Sand seems to get everywhere
In the strangest
Places
Sheets
Toes
Baths
Shorts
Pants
No
Matter what you do
You can't
Get rid of sand
If you have
Sex
There is sand there too
Personally I like
To wear 12 inch platforms
So that I have as
Little contact with
It as possible,
I like the look of it

From afar
But the idea of
Sweaty hot
Bodies
Does not
Fill me with lust
It reminds me of
Death
Dirt
Pyramids
Camels
And the best
In my dreams
Would be
An Arab
Galloping with
Long white
Robes and three
Daggers
On a chestnut
Stallion
That
Could
Be alluring
Sand blinds you
And there

You are lying
In peace
One
Moment
And the next, you
Have a tiny
Crab crawling
Up your legs
And some dreadful
Insect buzzing
Round your nose.
Instead add water
And turn it
Into cement
A man
Comes
To me
"Its great I
Went swimming
It was peaceful,
It was calm
Beautiful,
Nobody kissing
Three hours
Just myself on a
Beach"

The problem is what
About my Blackberry?
It'll have
Sand
In it and if that
Doesn't work,
Its the end of
The world
People
Just don't understand
That you
Could possibly
Hate it.
No
Birds on the sand
Jelly fish
Empty bottles
With some hopeless
Forgotten
Message,
Some fat woman in
A g-string
Blocking the view
Thomson
Holidays
And novels make it sound

So
Good
You are holding
Hands
Getting married
Collecting shells
Laughing, playing ball,
Eating
Now
There is a
Problem
Sand gets in
Your Pad Thai
All hell breaks
Loose and then
A pair of
Your friends
Salty, sandy oily
Boobs land
In your
Tom-yam-goong.
Then
People talk such
Rubbish in the sand
Reading Voici,
Hello

And old photocopies
Of The Daily Mail
Addles the brain
You start
To itch
And run
Hiding
With dreams of
A golden
Stallion
To hand
It could
Be good
On a windy
Wet English day
In
Some
Shabby long gone
Town.
Just reading
And writing
I am going to have
A bath right now.
Give me a sunbed anyday.
And the sea one mile
Away.

Your
Winning
Smile

Your winning
Smile
Is all but
Forgotten
Kiss my neck
Once more
And bring
Alive my
Skin
Breathe
Into my ears
And whisper
Sweet
Nonsense
And
Remember
The love
I have
For you...
Leave me
Breathless
Not alone
And take

Me to the
Dark caverns
Of your
Troubled
Brain
To drink
Your soul
But leave
Me free
To gallop
Along empty
Paths
And lonely
Trails
It is enough
To be
Forsaken
It is okay
Never shall
I Forget the
Beautiful
Bashful
Boy

How Skinny Are You

How skinny are you
Now darling one
Is your beautiful
Body
Starting to show
Are you becoming
A new creature
Ever changing
I hope so darling one
And can't wait
To see you
And stroke
And cuddle your
Brow

The Minute

The minute
You put useful
And practical
In the same sentence
It's a turnoff.
Maximalism
Is at
Least attractive
And
Minimalism
Is ugly,
Not practical
Practical shoes
Are a disaster
A practical haircut
Wash cut and run
Practical clothes
Geezer bird kit
Gurkha bird combat
Clothes
Just because
It's useful
It doesn't have to
Look ugly
A cheese grater
Can look beautiful
A knife too
A dustbin
Soap
A light bulb,
A CD
Hell to useful
Hell to practical.

Awake

Awake
Cannot sleep
A daunting
Task ahead
Allows no
Rest
In my head
A promise
Is a promise
And
I am
Prepared to
Fight
100 percent
It's just that
I am frightened
Have I made
A mistake?
Was everything
A crazy
Illusion?
Or was it real
Time will tell
And fate will
Show her hand
And be kind I
Hope
And understand.

Nature

I want nature
I need green
To learn to grow
Vegetables
As well as the
Love of concrete
I want to swim
In a stream
And go to Bhutan
To have earth under
My bare feet
To live in a
Misty shangri-la
The fog in my
Hair
The monks
Living there
To pray
And finger
Beads
With my forefinger
And thumb
Humming sounds
To a drum
I want serenity
To wear an apron
And to live in a
Nunnery.

COUTURE SHOW

Tissue
Silk
Swathed her
Face
A hat
Round the pool
Laughter
Her teeth
Red full lips red
The devil
Alive
Yet so angelic
Riding
Galloping through
Life
Her colourful
Sadness
Only a hint
Never believing
But believing
Her
In her hospital bed
Her feet
Broken
Crawling
I need a cigarette
But still
Seeing her by
The pool with
Couture
On her head

Running
And laughing
Gossiping
And he too
My friend
Now dead
Her screaming
"We can have fun"
"Had the knife again?",
Then serious
Then intellectual
Then mad
Then loyal
Disloyal
We all had memories
Her hats
Her crazy
One-off
Hats
And clothes
Trashed
And loved
Now gone
Her pheasant
Her cooking
Her fingers pounding
"I am going to
Die down the street
No-one will care
Or remember"
Her screech
Why can you
Have children.
Be rich

The men
The hats, hats, hats,
The chipped nails
The dirty
Scuffed loved shoes
The hair dryer
The caustic wit
The lipstick on her
Teeth
The vulgarity
Her coffin
Covered with lilies
And black beads
But
I remember you
Darling,
I just didn't believe,
You
But now you're
Dead,
And I'm left
With shivers
Running down
My neck
The asylum
For the living dead
The handbags given away
Expensive and unused
You are now an angel
I hope but
Inside I dread.

The
Membranes

Sensitive
The soft skin
Yielding
Fingers linger
Stop and hold
The lashes
Flutter
Carefully
Giving hidden
Pleasure
Lost in
Moments
Seeks
A hidden membrane
Not knowing
But knowing what
I am doing
Concentrating
I lick
And gently
Bite his lips
Swallowing
Wanting to be swallowed
And giving
Eating
If only I could eat
His sallow skin
Engulf him
With pleasure
No thought
But pleasure
Gasping toes curled
Longing
I watch
See his face
His chin raised
The veins
Alive

Whole hard
Slow and hard
Eyes closed
His hair
In my face
His smell
Real
Alive
I need to feel
Will he
Won't he
Hurt
Yes
I want to
Now be among
This bliss
Feeling
So free
Pure and
Demanding
Grabbing
And gently squeezing
Electricity
Shocks through my body
I want more
And
Need more
Body
Entering mine
Never ending
But ending
And then
Wishing
For the raw
Hard real core
Of his
Own being.

The Thorns

The thorns
With faded roses
Petals dropping
Like snowflakes
The door
Slightly open
But it no longer
Moved
I pushed and shoved
It no longer moved
The cobwebs
Of time
Handcuffed me
Stopped me from
Moving
Spiders working
Their way to heaven
The fabrics brittle
Moss
Of all types
Pale green
And dark
On the path
Of time
Daylight at the
End of a tunnel
So I could vaguely

See
Another alone
By a fire
Warming their
Gnarled hands
And sore feet
Before
The hot flames
Of tomorrow
Not a place for me
I needed light
And laughter
Wind and water
The sails flapping
Against the wind
Rather than sailing
Into it
The salt giving me
Blisters on my face
Waking me
Showing me eternal
Bliss
Of the silence and
Loneliness of the
Deep green
Sea.

Silence

When I don't hear
From you
I feel the air
Hitting my face
A sinking heavy
Air
That glues me to
A spot
I know why you
Are silent
I understand
And yet it makes
Me lost
Lost in a well
In a forest
At sea
In a boat
The silence and pain
I have
Is worth the
Times we share
You see they
Are a necessary

Sugar sprinkled
On my soul
A handbag
At your place
Some make up
Shoes lying carelessly
I like to prepare
For you my little
Hidden token
Of joy
A chocolate mousse
Eating wild strawberries
To live a dream
For a few
Minutes
In my life
With a man who
Is so perfect
In every way
That I had dreamt about
In youth
I had asked
God
Please send me

A tall, hook nosed man
With an artistic brain,
Long-legged
Who lives in an artist's
Studio
Why that I do not know
And
While watching films
I wanted to find
A Trevor Howard
Gregory Peck
A beautiful Hollywood
Man
So I am grateful
To the beings
Who helped out
Some hidden magical
Dust
Who made me
Wake up and
Notice
The creature
Whilst he slept.

Dancing On Candles

I left you
In a sea
Of candles
Dancing on mirrors
In a beautiful
Palace
Made for me
You kissed
Me as you
Should
And stroked
My thigh
I wanted more
And hungrily
Grabbed
Your tongue
Between my
Teeth
Stroking
Your face
Smoothing
Your wrinkled
Brow
You see I

Longed for your
Smiling
Face
In a sea of flames
Next to me
As
We lay down.
I wanted to suck
And kiss
And not
To forget
This star I had
Been sent
And not
Regret.
To love and enjoy
And love again
Putting my hand into
Hot water
And noticing
That
It feels cold
Before it burns.

Can He Take His Mask Off?

Can he take his
Mask off?
The lace and ribbon
Too
Can I take
Off mine?
The smoke the bluff
The vine
Would we like
Each other,
Why I ask
I do not
Know
Because
This I know is true.
And what would
We see?
But I see already
He thinks I don't,
I do
I'll take the risk...
I understand
He thinks I don't.

Too scared
Of life and change
And little things
Of batons scarves
And rings
The guilt, repulsion
The lust and love
And guilt
I have been to hell
And
Back
And thank God
For that
I have
Nothing to lose
I said everything I
Should
And all that I
Shouldn't too
I don't believe in
Hiding
Behind some
Fake old
Fabric

Romance

I want my
Hand
Held
Along
A beach
With dogs
Walking
Alongside
Well I think so
Anyway
It's a stupid
Thought
And I will
Like neither
By the end
To throw a stone
And make the
Bed
To take a child
To school
To hear them
Sing
To watch them
Act
Their first baby

Steps
This will make me
Laugh I think
But how wrong
I am
And how right
I am as well
I like passion
Change
And new men
Too
I like the
Smell of
Freedom
Of salty tears
And
Wind
Upon my face
My heart must
Beat
The thrill
Of the new
I must be
Kept alive
And race with time.

Twisted Wheel

I think
Long ago
Wrapped up in
White towels
In each other's
Arms kissing
Stroking
"Play for me
A little"
"Play for me
Please"
The tune
Unravels
Slowly
I move
Lying under
The piano
His fingers gliding
Nervously
Haunting, tragic
His feet
Elegant, long
I dream
Of a girl learning
Lines
For a play
Her life
Of hope.
Beautiful.
He makes me

Pine nuts and
Tomatoes
And later
Licks my arms
My body
Making love
In a most
Delicious way
He smells me
While she learns
Her lines and
Becomes a spy
And falls in love
Too and dies
Like a butterfly
I dream in early
Summer
He is in hell
I fly not knowing
Why
I just do
I fly and arrive
In a suburb
Not knowing where
I just do
Like a yellow
Happy bird
I listen
But I already knew
And I watched

The agony of
His face
The pain
The sound moves on
Against the rape
Of a young girl
The white flesh
Exposed, her hair
Arms
Alluringly visible
I listen to vultures
The old man's
House
His family, children, books
I hold and leave
As quickly
As I arrived
The young girl
Loved
And me?
Not sure
A pearl heart-shaped
Pendant given
But not for me
Couldn't love for a
Jewel
Deep retching
Angst
Of love

The tandem ride
The wheel turning
As she betrayed
His heartbeat
And mine too
So green
His touch
His words of love
While he loves
And she begins
And then dies
I photograph in Rome
But want to kiss
His sullen face
The year unfolds
The leaves have
Changed
The birds too
And still
Alive
Holding fingers
While she is
Dead
Her pendant pawned
Her wheel of fortune
Turned
And I
Touch the brow
Of this melancholic
Man.

Luke Warm

Luke warm
Water from a
Tap
Barely cleans
Me
I walk towards
The mountain
But no
Longer care
To understand
It doesn't make me
Excited
To chase on
Unwanted ground
Nothing opens
I shall not press
But all is dying
As He thinks of
Himself only
Nothing growing
He hates to share
Yet I remember
A swim by moonlight
And romantic
Thoughts
And dreams
All dissolved by sleep
As the cockerel
Of time
Awakes to give
Its news.

Pools Of Light

I hug my memories to me
Trying to capture
Small fragments
Of feeling
Remembering
Your skin and hair
Swimming in pools
Of light
Holding me in the
Water
Losing me
Holding me there
Dogs disturbing
The peace
Wanting to
Play
Lost in warm water
I try to hold you
In my arms
But you are not there
Scribbling over
My thoughts
I try to smile but
Cannot
Quiet please
Sssh... quiet so I can
Again listen to the
Water
And feel you against
Me once again.

Two Afternoons
I looked twelve afterwards
Two moments
Of bliss
With a man I like
The roses
No talking
Just sighs
Hated him going

Solitude

No longer caring
About the past
No longer miserable
So much calmer
Loving a little
Solitude
But not too much
I love the feeling
Of being touched
Held and kissed
Not for me to
Be on my own
Too long
Not for me
A bachelor
Life
Not for me

Washed Out Regret

Did I ever love
Did I ever feel
Was it real
The pain and
Torture
The sleepless
Nights
The bare bed
Hot and now so cold
Winter the leaves
Are gone
I long to be held
And now it's too late

So many vile
Things
Said
No
Sanity
I am a mad creature
A disused cloth
Of washed out regret
Trapped behind
Bars
A wild animal
Clawing at the ground
Crying to be heard

Sweaty ugly miserable
The leaves have gone
The birds no longer
Sing
A candle flickers
In the wind
A baby cries
The kettle sings
But I am dead
Tired from no
Sleep
And many pills
So tired

Sugar Meringues

I am going to dream about
Being pissed with you
Tomorrow
Night whilst eating
Happily I dreamt
About them last night
I was feeding you
Strawberry meringues
With cream
We were laughing in the
Soft mushy shells of
Fluffy delightful
Sugar and eggs
Whipped frothy
Cooked
We were
Feeding each other
Small portions
Of happiness
Allowing the sugar to
Coat our tongues
And melt our pain.

Good Times

Good times
Kiss the past
Behind
Colour it
Yellow
Like the tulips
From spring
And paint the
Town red with
Dancing
In the streets
And laughing
With good friends,
Holding hands
In the grass
And swimming
In a lake
Forget the rain
The pain
The dreary day
Today
The future is
Pink. Sprinkle
Your goodness
With words of
Kindness
And sparkle
Like the dazzling
Star you are
With humour and
Laughter
Remember just
The light and all
Will glow with
New thoughts
Caressing
The sky

THERE WAS A MEXICAN

"There was a Mexican you know"
I shuddered at his success
The hair removal cream
Staring at me in my face
The cruel words lashed through my heart - another time
"You are not the only one you know"
His beautiful looks diminished
Against the sun
"Between you and my wife"
I listened trying to ignore his insecurity
But never to forget him hiding behind the door
The two hours and twenty minutes of pleasure
He just gave and only gave
So keen to see me come
And equally for me to go
I asked if I could stay the night
"Oh please I have texts to do and write"
His face, he smiled
His real self realising and not realising
What he says will I win a Nobel Prize!
"My wife she doesn't understand"
"My lovely sparkling wife"
All I see is a wrinkled face the pointy finger time

Etched and standing still
"Use the code I can't see you every week"
I smile as if I do not hear
But I never forget the passion we had,
If only he did not speak
"I left my wife you know"
"I must show gratitude"
"Can you not shout, swear, or be yourself"
He lashes with serenity
Feeling my throat
To show me how to speak
In pretend ignorance I listen
But so in love I cannot see
I hear instead
"I love to fuck you, you make me hard"
"You are the best I ever have had in bed"
"You dress, you wear clothes nobody else can"
"I love your pins"
"I hate your pins"
The gentle massaging
"I want to hear you come"
The soft murmurings of making love
His true and real self.

Am I Miss Scarlet
In the cupboard?
Watch out
I could come out and stab you
To prove I do exist

Spy

I lay in bed for two
Days unable to
Move
My heart
Had crippled me
Left me incapable
Lonely
Unloved
Desired by no-one.
I wanted him
To love
Me
Not to treat
Me like the trash
He thought I was
I had made love
To him
Adored him
I wanted to be sick
To hold his
Hand
To be his
I want to make
The impossible
Possible
To never behave
Badly
Again
To be his

I want to be able to
Do it
Please God help me
Please
If I get this man
Please give me
The strength to
Love
To be loved
I cry for fears
That may not happen
Will I get dumped
Will I ever find anybody else
The door slams
And I am told
It's not a relationship
You're not in a
Relationship
If only I had a gun
But then
I carry only lipsticks
And mobiles
Tarted up
With a beret
To hide feelings
Looking like a spy
I leave the
Room.

The L-Shaped Room

I am just about to
Sleep and thought
About you in Porchester
Square when I loved
You so much
And when I left
You in despair
The L-shaped room
I forgot
The passion
I had
The endless
Fish and chips
And pizzas on
Tuesday nights
The odd
Sneaky weekend
In Paris
The visits to
The flea market
And the Chatelet
The endless arguments
And no regret
The rare holidays
Together
Cuba
Ten fake watches
Capri
I wanted to create
The furniture I made
By hand
Lovingly I assembled
Each and every piece
The pink pillows

The white walls
Stark and beautiful
The bath you
Could open all its
Walls and talk and
Laugh then
Leaving I would
Come back
Unable to say
Good bye
One last kiss
Please
Before the cold air
Touched my lips
And cheeks
I lovingly
Kissed you
I was merrily your slave
In the stark white
Rooms chained
Do you remember
The mice
Running over the
Floors dancing
Trying to
Catch them
Playing in my sleep
Why? I don't know
So excited to
Create a love story
From my past
One day
I got caught
And after one or two

Years I locked the doors
Of my heart
For a haven I once had
With six huge windows
A secret hiding place
Revealed.
Sleeping, no time to
Sleep, as I stroked and
Tickled your back
One last time
Never could it be
The same again.
Never could I feel
The same
I loved you there
And then
Well I really
Loved you only then
So desperate
For you to love
Me
So dead
The L-shaped
Room
The only happiness
We had
Fallen to the wrinkle
Of the brain
Domesticity
Where is the brown curly
Hair turned grey?
The cheeky face
Has it hidden its
Charm?

No Bit, No Reins

He arrived through
The stable door
No bit, no reins
His mouth free
With a certain
Brightness and
Determination in his
Mouth
Firm, sleek and fit
No fear
His black mane
Flowing in the wind
Waiting in the wings
To mate his mare
Cold
Fresh from the
Outside paddocks
And he had freedom
There
He spoke to me
Throwing the dust
Up under his hooves
Switching his tail
Neighing to me
Across the yard
He knew I would be

There
Often we met
When galloping through
The park
Through the meadows
We raced
Rearing and prancing
And
Later
He would bite gently down
My spine
His nostrils meeting
Mine
His mouth full of oats
And hay
Always faithful always
There
I would roll in the stable
The fresh straw
Soothing my excited
Skin
In the night we opened
Our stable doors
Taking flight secretly
Against the freezing
Air.

Dead Values

Looking at the floor
He could hardly move
Vile hard faced
Shocked that
He no longer
Loved her
The woman he had
Fought so hard
To get.
Her pointy finger
And grating voice,
Nagging,
Never stopped
In his head.
He studied himself
In the mirror.
Good-looking, firm
Young, clean skin
Handsome.
Why didn't she
Think so too?
Why was she so
Unhelpful?
Why did she no
Longer make love?
Why didn't she look

After herself,
Make herself attractive
For him?
Why didn't he fancy
Her?
All she believed in
Was the box the very
Small box of left wing
Values: equality, sharing
Hard work, hers as
Important as his.
He realised he had
Changed, grown, explored
And could no longer be
Trapped in the small
Town life.
He needed a big city,
Excitement, a successful
Career, stardom –
Anything but the dull
Ordinary life of a wife
He had grown tired of.
Taking a closer look,
He realised
There was nothing wrong
With him.
And everything wrong
With her.

He just didn't believe it.
The woman he married had
Been his shining star,
An angel, a holy creature
Beautiful. Loving,
Given him children
She had done everything
For him.
Now she screamed and
Yelled; her jealousy
Left her in a heap
On the floor
She had tried
To capture him
But instead had hit
Him over the head with an
Air conditioning unit.
Blood flowing out of
Him.
Facing his bruise he
Wanted to leave.
He couldn't
His fingers covered
With marks.
She had scratched
Like a cat.
By the bed the bank
Statement lay

She had spent so much
On underwear
He never saw.
Horrified but saying nothing
He washed
His face
And started to
Work,
Closing the door
So he no longer
Heard her.
Gradually
Breathing a sigh
Of relief he opened
His emails while the
Blood pumped through
His veins
She had to go.
He would make
Her.
But he had to look
Clean so he could
Withdraw and hide
And sleep and run
And work.
Until she cried
Again.

The Fury, The Fear

The fury
The fear or loneliness
The fear of no
Money
Money less
Clueless
The emptiness of life
Fear of freedom
Manipulation
Too much
Information
Greed
Need
Fuzzy brain
Wanting a clean
Can you clean it
Like a car?
Why
Why not my brain
Needs a clean
Ajax
Spite
Perversity
Of shitty
Power
Why
The power of
It
Magnificent
The power of pride
Amusement
Of shitty shittiness
I'm alive or dead
Dead or alive
The fear of both
Nothing is fear
Fear is nothing

Virgin Bride

Cake smeared
All over
The mirror
Imprints on
The sheet
Particles of
LUST
Lipstick
Evidence
Of grotesque past
Desire.

It's Funny

Its funny I feel I
Should have
Feelings
But they
Drifted away
Like a scar
It drives you
Mad
So painful
Then suddenly it's
Gone.
I often think
Of how they went
The slow process
I had no
More love
Left
Just a cruel
Laughter to
Torment.

Stones & Bottles

A dust bowl heat
Boiling hot unable
To breathe
She travelled
Through Lebanon
Her country
Up in
Fire and smoke
Noticing
A little boy
Playing with a
Plastic bottle
In rags
Blood
On his hands
People still managing
To plant their
Vegetables
Just, happy,
Scraping to live
No telephones
Remote
A strike for

300 dollars
A month turns
Into tyres burning
Twenty-five
Hairy men
Jumping on her car
With sticks, guns,
And stones
They whip the mirrors,
The windows
Trying to
Grab her
Her driver trying
To calm his brothers,
Her fellow men
A man with a bag
Of potatoes
Asked for help
She cried in the
Dust ridden car
Please help
Screamed through tears
Streaming down

Her face
Holding the flower,
Her favourite
Flower, her mother
Gave her, now wilting
In her sweaty palms
Men trying to
Preserve the borders
Of their beautiful
Country
They drive through
The distressed rabble
With knives, wood, bottles
Furious and desperate
Unable to bury their
Dead
Little children running
In the streets
A woman dying
Killed for buying
Bread.
The other side
In high heels

Buying caviar
With their
Mercedes, no
Thoughts but their
Bodies and
Manicured nails,
Damaged by excess
All in the same situation
Though
War makes love
More strong
The day the borders
Closed
My friend knew what love
Meant,
Whom you love
And who
Are willing to die for.
Vomiting with fear she bribes
Her way out,
Terrified forlorn
She leaves her paradise.

Delicately

Delicately
I took
Rose petals
Pink and fading in the
Early morning
Light
And sprinkled them
On
The bed
I lit a candle
On the desk
Early
So its scent
Filled the room
I chose
My lover's food
Carefully
Knowing he doesn't
Eat

Strawberries,
Blueberries
And some wild honey
So happy to see him
When he arrived
I pulled him close
To me
To remember his
Breath
To kiss his face
And stroke
His ears
To hear him speak
Softly his sweet
Words
Whispering sweet nothings
Down my spine
As I arch it
Just for him.

The Choir

The choir
Singing in an
Icy church
Freezing
My breath
Cold
Against the
Chorus of their
Voices
All boys
Believing.
Holy against
The hell of blasphemy
The wrath of God
The conductor
Waving his hands
Happy to
Grip his wand
The boys forgetting
Their fights

Detention
Pure, hoping not
To be.
Damnation will
Grip their souls
But not yet,
Still locked up
Behind gates
Away from
Women, drugs
And drink
The incense
The smell of boys
Behind them,
Believing
That they are
The only ones to have
Existed
Tidy in their tails
Good-looking
Young innocent faces

Their truths to yet
Unfold
My son
Relaxed
Ready to sing
Beautiful
Against the
Strings
In German
His pure voice
Repels my demons
The horns
The boys quietly
Gossiping
Whispering
Delivering
Us from evil
But creating it
And planning it
For the future.

One By One The Petals Fell

One by one the
Petals fell
Like snow
Tiny
Beautiful
In time
To the flute
And as if by
Magic
Following the
Sound
They danced
Along in
The summer
Evening
The squirrels
With their bushy
Tails watched
The rabbits
Too
Gingerly following
Then skipping

The fox and her cubs
Had no such
Hesitation
Along the hedgerows
In and out of the
Hay
Happy to be safe
Following
The man with his
Flute dancing by
By dusk the bees
The sparrows
Robins
Magpies
Three little
Girls with cups
And long blonde hair
Laughed
As they threaded
Daisies
Making tiny
Necklaces
Noticing

The angel with
His flute
In the summer
Air
As the grass
Became wet
The boy
With his long
Black hair
Lay down
On some wood
Perfect in
Every way
And was adorned
With flowers
And wild fruits
The cups, the
Girls, all nude
The birds the bees
All sang sweetly
To this god
From the sky

I Know
What Love Is,
I've Had It
Sometimes

Today's date is a day
Nearer the end than
I thought
It was.
Thinking about it,
I am
Really
Stinky today,
And I don't care.
I am a depressing
Old cow.
I can only do ordinary
For five minutes
But as the seconds
Tick tock
It's beige
I want to scream.
I have food on my pulley
I look as if,
Oh no, plates are being
Broken next door,
You see it's like
Wading in treacle, with
Margarine down the door
Salmon on the floor
I want to explode
And I can't.

Please tell God
I want to be a guinea
Pig, give me the drugs,
It hurts.
You know
I know what love is
I have had it sometimes
Running in the rain
Kissing under an umbrella with
Dead spiders in my
Pockets.
You can tell the difference
When you know the
Difference.
You can't have second-hand love,
Its all there is.
A girl's at my door
She has teeth like a
Row of condemned
Houses,
If they really don't
Want to know...
What love
Is.
Then I can't, help them.
Take your man
He has the currency

Called Dosh.
He thinks
I am the God of
Dosh.
You can afford it
But what is it for?
Although he has the
Money, what's it all for?
Clearly insecure?
Your arsehole is not
Hung with diamonds.
I want to be in
Cape Cod
And
Pretend somebody
Is everything you
Want them to be.
"The french beans
Are a little hard
Darling"... It's your
Turn to be the maid now.
My eyeball sees things
That no
Private jet can,
There's no
Tour guide
And you can't

guarantee
To go there
Again.
If I can see the difference
Between
The
Real and fake
Balenciaga
Then I want the real
Not the fantasy.
I am not falling
Down as much.
You know
I sat in my bedroom for three
Nights crying.
In my present condition
I qualify for 13 reality
Programmes from
The House Doctor to
Big Brother.
When I ask is anybody
There
A little voice
That Says "No"
If you can only
Understand

One in five
Lines
I am not interested
In you.
No demon
Seed on the
Carpet please.
I went out with
A midget once
He had a double
Set of hearing
Aids on, but could
Only hear, from
The vibrations...
I am going to douche
Now
My stinky, stenching
Limbs with cheap
Scent.
God's taking the piss.
I smell of old Teddy
Bear.
Half of me wants to go
And have a sunbed
And some highlights
And half wants to
Close the curtains

And drag them across
All the things on the
Shelf.
When checked by
My neighbours
I have two fingers
Ready,
My tits hanging out
For a fireman
To come and
Rescue me.
I have come
To realise,
What I have come
To realise.
And remember as one
Door closes,
Another slams on your
Fingers,
Its always darkest
Before it goes
Completely black,
Forget about Dawn
She's hawking
Her wares up the
Edgeware Road.

Right Or Wrong

Is it gutless to stay
Or
Is it gutless to leave
I could not have
Loved him
If he wasn't
Extremely
Sensitive
That is what
I believed
But
The thought
That his Mother
Is dying and he
Doesn't react
The thought that
His son is sick
And
He doesn't come home
Another son

He never sees
He's not interested
Yet he ties me
I cannot
move
He loves me
However flighty
I am
He knows
I am dependable
He never comes
I wonder if I am to blame
I made him into
This
I think it's very
Difficult
To be totally honest
And say this doesn't
Work.

Royal Path

Along the path
I walked in awe
Of all I saw
The wooden
Stumps of time
Where lilies grow
The fountains
Poured and the
Birds flew
Two bronze storks
Stand
Surrounded by moss
Earth, ivy
Catching small
Particles of light
I stepped lightly
Into a bewitching
Tunnel of leaves
With the beauty of
The promiscuous oak

Strong a king among
Kings
And Monkey puzzle
Trees confusing all
I saw a butterfly
An Emperor
Whose superiority among insects
Flies by
Along my magical
Road
Eucalyptus leaves
Brush my hand as
I walk barefoot
Gliding over moss covered
Paths long forgotten
I wanted to be
Alone and sit
And think listening
To a bird
Calling for a friend
To watch

The light changing
Like small diamonds
Making daylight
Turn to night
I touch the Imperial
Bench
But dare not sit
Instead
I lie on stones
Imagining fairies
Washing their wings
I long for you to
Stroke and place
Your hands,
Holding my hands
And hiding me among
The golden primulas
And ferns
I long to be cold
With you
And you alone.

Mmmmmmm
I didn't want to leave this Morning
I was curled up like
A cat
Happily purring
Beside you
I really love
Cuddling you
I wish there wasn't a curfew
And I could
Spend some time
With you

Ice Green Confection

I am not
Comfortable
In the space
Of others
Their silence
And noise
Their books
Unread
Their perfect
Leather
White sofas
The mingling
The fake talk
The glass
Their parties
The alcohol

It looks attractive
An iced green
Confection
Of something
Lime and lemon
But it's not
The hidden
Drugs
Nobody tells
Me about
Leaves me
Dark and lonely
On a stool
And smile
And sit and watch
Yet I go
And know

There will be
Two second
Hellos
And yet I go
And relinquish
The
Warmth of my
Pink sofa
My pink and gold
Flowery room
For the
Emptiness
But visual
Beauty of
Another's
Hollowness

A Gritty Tale

A birthday ball
At a stately home
I am sure they
Would love to know
Who wrecked their
Country seat
The Peacocks in
The garden
And the fat cats
In the house
Five four three
Two one
They refused to
Kiss her when they
Left
She blow dried her hair
Afterwards
It looked perfectly
Alright
Fabulous pictures
Just a little touch
Up with the
Make up

It takes somebody
To be detached
Anybody who could
Work under the pressure and
Light.
Very young
Funny and I keep trying
To find her
Under the lights,
She is there
Somewhere.
It's true, I look
For her.
He paid the
Models as little
As possible.
"I can't do that"
She would do it.
He did two to five minute
Videos with them
Up by the cemetery,
A girl said make
Me look gorgeous,
I think

Where is my friend
I hear her smashing
Up plates in the kitchen,
She sounds like she's
Cooking for fifty
To make one cup of tea.
The girls came from
The job centre.
She's brain dead
Too pretty and classy
For that.
I endure her to remember
Her,
As she was before
But she's gone
I sometimes get
A glimpse,
She had fragility
Almost a virgin
Quality isn't it?
To play with dollies.
What do the pictures
Look like?
Patch it up

On the outside but
It is deceiving...
Underneath she
Nearly died.
The only pleasure
She had was when
It ended
The only feelings
Were for shopping
I put her in laundry
Starch to make her
Look good.
Girl, look sharp
I wrung out sheets
In icy weather
I was experimented
On
How can I be shocked
By anything?
That is why I look
For her,
And tidy her up, and
Make her look alright.

Pebbles Between My Toes

Don't let me
Walk your drive
To feel pebbles
Underfoot
To hurt
My toes
To drive
To see
A happy face
That's all I want
Don't pretend
To be correct
To let
Me down so
Gently with your
Tongue
I understand
The duality
Of life

The Onion Man

Every time I check
I find one more layer
One layer makes
Me Cry
A packet of Tampax
In a cupboard
I grit my teeth and
As I peel unknowingly with
My earthy fingers
They sting
And my open sores
Weep
One strip
Can be sweet
I smile
And I keep my mouth shut
Who used the hair removing
Cream?
A jar of Vaseline?
I don't search so I
Don't find
But always there's
Another layer to shock
And maybe please
The onion is
Both delicious and
Repellent

I believe him when he kisses
My tummy in the
Morning light
Earthy and delicate
Both necessary yet
Hidden
A box of foie gras
Given lovingly,
Is given away
Carelessly,
Throw away lines
Hurt and
Pierce my spirit
As my insides
Shudder
But still I carry
On peeling to find the
Inner core,
I rub my eyes
But can't see clearly,
I have jealousy
I can feel it,
I hate myself,
But no more
Than the pain
Of finding Durex oil
In some pale
Blue plastic jar

With £2.99 beside a bed
I take a knife
And go to another
Place
And clean it
Thoroughly
Lady Macbeth comes
To my mind,
The more I scrub
The dirtier it
Becomes
My eyes can't
Move now,
The bitter sweet
Juices enter through
The soft tissue.
I see a car in
A drive
The telephone rings
Unknown
As I peel and peel
With hope
That I have a flower
In my hand
And not this ordinary
Vegetable,
A rose maybe
But that will have thorns

Too.
I must
Be careful,
Not to see the Viagra
In the pocket
Of his vest
So the erections
Are also
Counterfeit?
I hope to find a bottle
Marked compassion
Inside,
Instead of something
That says, swallow this,
But this is
An empty bottle.
Swallow this and tell
Me this.
Don't go I have some
More lies to tell to
You
Artichokes have
Hearts.
And celery too.
Please don't lie to me
Any more
It will make me lie to you
Even less

The Movie Star Dream

She knows how to wear drops instead of diamonds
She knows how to wear flats
She knows how to wear dirty clothes and look a star
She loved sex so she escaped the movies
She was
Very boring underneath
Born in a trash can
And funny
She was tormented
You know
What I like about movie stars is the drugs
They drop from their bedside tables
It is not because you
Wouldn't
It is not because
You shouldn't
A little more décolleté
She changed five times
On the plane
Dropping alcohol on
The floor
She clapped
Can you kiss me
Men did
It gave her freedom
It made her look like she used La Prairie you see,
Women have a lot of problems
Between
Stilettoes and
"I haven't eaten all day".

Real & True

"You can get copies
Of Agent Provocateur
Down the high street."
The wet and nasty
Mindy said on her razor
Phone.
She hated the idea
Of old age
Creeping all over her.
He had overly white
Dentures
Every time he smiled
Everybody put
Their Raybans on.
Mindy could fool
The planet
With her fake Prada
Bag.
Real imitation plastic
Cannot be
Distinguished
From the real
Thing.
But she never had
Seen the real

Thing.
If she saw the real
She said it was
Counterfeit.
Mindy had the skin
Texture of double
Cheese with extra
Topping, she covered
This with fake tan.
Neon plastic flowers
In her hair, and fake
White nails
Mindy was almost
Pretty.
She found a book
On runes
Under her stale sandwiches
She made my friend
Read it out
Mindy told me
I didn't have
Enough red in my
Love chakra.
Her boyfriend had smoothed
His hair over
In a sort of

Bouffant hair-do
He was going bald
And was the victim
Of some stuff called
"Mane" too black
On blonde fine hair.
Mindy was boasting
She bought some earrings
She said they were
Real
But they turned
Her ears green
They put her on
Antibiotics for a
Week, she had
Boasted they made her lose
Eight pounds
She wanted me to buy
Them from her
She did seven costume
Changes in twenty minutes
Until she was down
To nothing
She sang Carmen Miranda
I like you very much
Please don't clap

They mostly clapped
In the wrong
Places
I'm offered a fondant finger
The type they make
Trifle with
Sneering at me
With one gold tooth
I had to leave
She wanted me
To sign her immigration
Application form
I sort of scribbled
My name
She could hardly speak
A word of English
She kept saying
How many benefits
She could get
Grabbing at a fondant
I took myself
Out into the fresh
Air with a hotdog and
Thought how to
Buy some time.

165

Dolly

Would he love me
If he realised I was
Assembled
Like a dolly
In a factory
Made up and coloured
As a Hollywood
Film star
The lashes
The minute
Brush strokes
The painful
Routine in a gym
Would he love me
If he knew I took
A dictionary to
Bed to feed my
Brain
Like scales upon
A piano to stretch
The small cells
Of grey matter
Would he love me
If he knew the books
I read
The old romantic
Novels
The dusty books
Hidden on a shelf

The wallpaper in my
Bedroom pink and gold
Would he love me
If he knew I only wore
Black
To hide my hidden
Self
Colour feeds the sorrow
Of a broken heart
Would he love me
If he knew
The pain he gave
To me
If only he knew
Would I still be desired
If they witnessed
Me at dawn being
Compiled of collagen
Stitching, microwaved,
Shrink-wrapped into
Pseudo-youth.
The hair blonde, shining
Silky, shampooed, slick
Ready to dive between
The sheets
Like a perfect mermaid
Dolly.
He desires
Me now.

Excite Me

Excite me
Tell me
What you are doing
Show me a fantasy
The way to wonderland
Tell me tell me
The ten-inch booties
A corset
Blonde ringlets
Tell me
What you do
Show me
Me
With your fingers
Help me
Suck me,
Lick my spine
Help
The wet
Red lipstick
A tissue
Nipples erect
Oil
Tell me
Speak to
Me whisper
Your dreams
Murmur
Softly blow
Sigh
The lace between

My legs
Finger me
Here
No
There
Feel my
Tightness
Plunge
Make me despair
Use your trickster
Tongue
Blindfolded near to
Hell
The incense
A scented candle
Press
My stomach
Let me scream
Have no
Regrets
Rip my stockings
Eat me now
Let me dream
And tell me now
With pearls
Between
My legs
And let me reach
Another plane
Without
Regrets and pain.

The Nosey Nose

Love
The sensitive
Rosy Nose
Old
Holy
Sacred
Organ
To treat
With respect, in
Gardens.
Never misleading
You if you listen.
It will show you
The Love of
Dandelions and
First thoughts,
That are in
The nose
The tulips.
The lilies.
Never again
Lying in a bed
Of nettles
Of no
Feeling

The transparent
Line of hatred
Stems
The desire
And hatred
Again
Leaves
Me cold.
I should have
Listened to
My nose.
Pure nose
Pure love
With no
Money attached
And cared for
My thoughts
The deep
Tunnel thoughts,
They are the only
Thing you can
Listen to and
Trust
The grassy satire
Pressure,

Religion,
People,
The cross,
Work.
Remember
The fields.
I should have
Watched more,
Thought
More:
Free of convention,
Free of religion,
Free to be who I wished
To be.
Earlier dreaming of
Snowdrops.
Nothing
Should
Match
But
The
Nosey nose
Of an
Edwardian
Bouquet

Don't Let Me

Don't let me
Walk your drive
To feel pebbles
Underfoot
To hurt
My toes
To drive
To see
A happy face
A loving dog
To cuddle
To love
That's all I want
Don't pretend
To be correct
To let
Me down so
Gently with your
Tongue
I understand
The duality
Of life
The meaningless
And do we exist
We don't

But we do
The only real feelings
Are the hands
Of children
Their nails
Their
Baby teeth
The love
We give and the
Deep thrusting
Passion of nights
Of bliss
The loving hands of
A woman who
Loves
The happy smile
She gives
Sometimes
People come to
Our lives and only
Later we know why
The path is trodden
Do not despair
All hands and love
Are there.